The Backwater Sermons

The Backwater Sermons

Jay Hulme

CANTERBURY
PRESS
Norwich

© Jay Hulme 2021

Published in 2021 by Canterbury Press
Editorial office
3rd Floor, Invicta House,
108–114 Golden Lane,
London EC1Y 0TG, UK
www.canterburypress.co.uk

Canterbury Press is an imprint of Hymns Ancient & Modern Ltd
(a registered charity)

Hymns Ancient & Modern® is a registered trademark of
Hymns Ancient & Modern Ltd
13A Hellesdon Park Road, Norwich,
Norfolk NR6 5DR, UK

British Library Cataloguing in Publication data

A catalogue record for this book is available
from the British Library

978-1-78622-393-7

Typeset by Regent Typesetting

Contents

Poem Order

Introduction

I often speak of being a 'Plague Christian' – I found God in November 2019, having been brought up so Atheist that at 23 I didn't know what date in December Christmas Day was. And soon after, a global pandemic changed the world.

Despite spending my entire life feeling drawn to churches and cathedrals, I'd spent years in denial, certain that I was too poor, too queer, too dodgy, to even enter them, let alone belong in them. Even after plucking up the courage to step inside, I'd tell myself that the sense of joy and peace I kept feeling in and around churches was just down to my appreciation of their architecture.

Finally, after meeting and befriending Real Life Christians (who just happened to be queer), a few more years of denial, and a dramatic and honestly miraculous incident involving Durham Cathedral, a boy, a bridge and an impossible moment of survival, I finally admitted God was real. I stole a Bible, phoned one of my Christian friends in a panic, was gifted more Bibles that were less obscure and outdated translations than the one I'd nicked, and read them cover to cover. Repeatedly.

A few months after that, Covid changed the world forever. In a dark piece of irony, all of the Church of England churches closed. I, a man who had found God through these physical buildings, was stuck, alone, in a room, with no connection to Christianity aside from some Bibles, and the phone numbers of the four Christians I knew – all of whom lived in distant cities which were suddenly illegal to visit.

Leicester was hit hard. Our lockdown never really ended. As I write this, it's been ongoing for over a year. Dozens of my friends, Atheists faced with Christian grandparents who were dying alone, began asking me, the only Christian friend they had, to pray for them.

When the pandemic began, I was supposed to be writing another book of children's poetry. Instead I found myself writing this. And as the pandemic rolled on, I realised that though it is possible to be Christian alone – it is indescribably hard.

I scoured the internet for a queer-friendly church and found St Nicholas' Church – the oldest church in Leicester, built in AD 879, and radically inclusive. I emailed the priest, asking how I would go about joining the church during a pandemic. She didn't know. I didn't know either. The church remained closed, even for private prayer. We'd meet up in parks, when it was legal, and talk about faith. I learnt to find God everywhere – not trapped in church buildings, but in every inch of earth. When St Nicholas' finally opened again in September 2020, I was there.

On the 24th of October 2020, I was baptised in that tiny ancient church. Many of my loved ones couldn't attend, so I asked online if people would light candles for me. Thousands of people from all over the world did, people from countless religions, and none. When my priest signed me with the cross at my baptism that was the first, and, to date, only, time a member of St Nick's and I have ever touched.

Soon, the churches closed again. I continued to find God in the ruined factories and polluted canals of this city. I discovered that God is just as present here, among the death and the urban decay, as They are in the astounding beauty of the grand cathedrals and open countryside that it was suddenly illegal to visit.

Among the struggles, and the closure, I was welcomed into St Nick's. Over time I was brought onto committees; given keys to the church; asked to show contractors around when we needed repairs. The poems in this book were arranged on the floor in front of the altar – poems laid out before God in an empty church.

This collection reflects the pain, and the beauty, and the strange perspective I have gained through being a 'Plague Christian'. Of having to find God everywhere, and in everything, during a time of incredible difficulty. Of seeking grace in agony, and finding it in abundance. Of calling out to God in anguish, and being comforted by limitless love. Of the beauty, and possibility, and wonder that can be found – even in such terrible times.

March 2021

Isaac

The Lord
does not ask
for that which
is easy

nor takes
that which
is too much
to bear

Take These Words

Having come to God in the closing phase
of my secondary adolescence, I find myself wondering:
At what point did my prayers become real?
At what point did my wordless pleas to unnamed deities
become something more than back-alley
begging to a bargain basement belief system, built on
bad behaviour, bad attitudes, and brokenness?

If I were to ask a priest, I think they'd say they were
always prayers, even when I didn't pray them;
that God was always waiting, in the silence.

Perhaps this is a prayer too – even this;
perhaps poems are just prayers, in their way.
We offer up the edge of things, and say:

Take this, take all of this.
Take these words that I have found
in the wilds of creation.

On Realising God Exists

The sky is falling and nobody has noticed,
there are chunks of it everywhere, with sharp edges.

Slabs of solid air and glints of light; not blue
like you'd expect, but simply shining.

A jogger steps on a piece and it splinters,
with shards of the sky on her trainers, she carries on.

I want to gather it up in armfuls and put it back,
but there's cracks all over the clouds and I think it's too late.

Between the edges of one patch of sky and another
I see darkness, and shafts of light.

The sky is falling and nobody has noticed.
There's something set behind it we cannot quite reach.

'Now you're Christian, do you pray and all that?'
and please can you pray for my nan?

I, accidental representative of a dying religion,
am kneeling for the thousandth time today,
asked by unbelievers to say:

                       God,
if these strangers must die,
                    let them die well.

England, the Twenty-Fifth of April 2020

Flowers are falling from the trees again,
  as they have every year since my birth.
   They fall without witness,

   petals congregate in gutters,
    pink and white in the dust.
     Flowers of flesh and bone.

If a tree blooms by the roadside, with nobody around
to see it, was it ever beautiful? And if a loved one
dies in a hospital, with nobody allowed to visit, will
the world remain bearable? And if their funeral is
attended by none but the vicar, can you truly wish
them goodbye?

A boy walks out of his garden,
  always watching for death
   in the form of a neighbour;

   his eyes fracture at the edges,
    spinning off into other realities,
     creating undefined worlds.

In the 1900s, scientists found that a baby monkey,
given a choice between a wire 'mother', who could
feed it, and a cloth 'mother', who could provide
nothing but touch, would choose to starve, every time,
in return for that touch.

The world is paused.
  Death stalks the streets on wisps of breath.
   Our homes are our refuge and our jailers.

   We consume ourselves, in the interim,
    slipping sideways with tiny footsteps,
    away to the edges of things.

5

Towpath Bodies

Tell me about every dream you've ever had;
perhaps start with the one filled with bodies.
Tell me how we pulled them from the canal.
How we lined them up on the towpath,
                              with pennies for eyes;
how you cursed the skies until it rained —
until you stopped the sun and the endless decay,
how it washed away the stench of it,
until even this water seemed clean.

Metaphors

We're living through a plague, but the plague is a metaphor,
and our loved ones are dying, and their deaths are metaphors,
and I write all these poems, and the poems are metaphors,
and the sun is so bright, and its brightness is a metaphor,
and the sky is a metaphor, and the lockdown is a metaphor;

and I call my boyfriend, and the phone is a metaphor,
the screen is a metaphor, the space is a metaphor,
and I cry at night, and my tears are metaphors,
on my cheeks, which are metaphors,
and the birds are metaphors, and their songs are metaphors,
and the news is a metaphor, about a government that's a
   metaphor;

we are all metaphors, in a world made of metaphors.
Nothing is itself, in times such as these,
we drown in implications, while trying to breathe
                                  — and that, too,
                                       is a metaphor.

Sketches from an English Summer, 2020

There are flowers blooming in the hedgerows;
birds sing in the sunlight of a summer morning;
a family gathers around a barbecue;
smoke fills the air like the echo of an endless siren.

There will be no rain this week, or the next.
No work either. The dry earth soaks up
spilled beer from a dozen illicit parties.
The ground is greedy, and desperate, and cracking.

This is the summer of too many endings,
of too many sudden goodbyes – but it is still the summer.
We gather our loved ones close in the blinding sunlight,
and cough as the smoke fills our lungs.

A Boy, Fleeing Death

There is a boy on my street
who rides a bicycle;
every morning, rides a bicycle.
Face tipped to the wind,
flushed with fear, and joy,
and the ecstasy of living.

Every so often he cycles up,
right up, to the top of the hill,
and careens downward.
Mouth ripped open, but silent,
as if he's trying to swallow
the world – or rebuke it.

Yesterday I saw him stop,
at the top of the hill, stop
and look out at the city.
I think he was waiting for a siren.
Flashing lights on the ring road.
The signal to start his fall.

Pete

He's mowing the lawn again,
the grass has a grade one cut
and it's time for a trim.

After every pass he returns to the house,
leans up against the conservatory,
stares at the lines in the grass,
and struggles to breathe.

His wife speaks to him, sometimes.
You're killing yourself, she says,
it's just a lawn, she says,
take a rest.

But the sun is shining,
and the grass keeps growing,
and today – today he is still alive.

A Very British Pandemic

I saw then the street,
and the street was filled with Death,
and the street was Death.

And Mrs Gold from round the corner
            (with the two pomeranians)
was a carrier,
and the pomeranians were carriers,

and the air was a carrier,
and it floated behind her –
this cloud.

She raised her hand in greeting
as she passed by,
four feet at most from the fence.

And so I smiled at Death,
as she walked the length of the pavement,
small white dogs
yapping away at her heels.

The Only Shop Still Open

The funeral parlour's busy these days;
the undertaker, still dressed in black,
slips in and out of the side.

Sometimes he spots a stranger,
a couple or two in the street
as he heads to the hearse.

Each time he looks up
and nods politely,
as they smile and wave in return.

We'll take care of you, too,

his eyes seem to say;
soft, and sad,
and seamed at the edges,

we'll take care of you, too,
when the time comes.

Anatomy of an Ending

Two shoes, laid neatly by the side of the bed,
dark brown, well polished, curling up a little at the toe;

a notepad full of sudoku puzzles,
most completed, correctly, in dark blue ink;

a half-empty bottle of Chanel no.5,
your wife's, though she died fourteen years ago;

your hand, reaching down to the carpet,
wedding ring on, palm open and beckoning.

Don't Die

I say it so often it's embedded in my skin.
$$\textit{don't die}$$
Have another cup of tea.
Did you buy the new shoes?
What's your plan for tomorrow?
$$\textit{don't die,}$$
$$\textit{don't die,}$$
$$\textit{don't die}$$

When the plague is over, we'll go dancing;
I hate dancing, but we'll go.
$$\textit{don't die}$$
We'll visit that coffee shop, if it's still open;
that one you took me to, before all of this.
$$\textit{don't die}$$

What's on telly?
$$\textit{don't die}$$
What're you eating?
$$\textit{don't die}$$
What do you want from this stunted existence?
$$\textit{please} \qquad \textit{don't die}$$

I'm reaching out again,
trying to find the edges of you in the ether.
A hundred miles away, and still beside me.

Let me tell you about the future.
                              don't die
What we're going to do together.
                              don't die

The supermarket is closing soon,
you have to go and buy groceries.
Be careful, I say.
                    Stay safe, I say.
          don't die
I say.
          don't die

Not a Poem

A poem in which I am kneeling at an altar,
giving all I cannot say to God.

A poem which is not a poem,
because these are not words.
A poem in which I am begging,
a poem in which I weep.

A poem in which my hands are clasped
so tightly together, my fingernails
make crescents in my skin.

A poem in which the candles have burned down,
in which the priest paces politely,
in which the silence is endless.

A poem in which the churches are not closed,
a poem in which all of this is possible;
a poem in which God listens.
A poem in which I do not speak.

Pandemic Prayers

Thank you God for the video call,
for the wi-fi connection,
for the 4G that's left on my phone.

Thank you God for the distance,
for the empty pavements,
for the two meters in between.

Thank you God for the housing,
for the roof and the walls,
for the bed.

Thank you God for the food bank. for the supermarket.
for the internet. for the livestream. for the tv show. for the
phone call. for the radio. for the book. for the face mask.
for the hand wash. for the soap. for the shower. for the
doctors. for the families. for the loved ones. for the money.
for the clean towels. for the pot plants. for the flowers. for
the soil. for the laundry. for the patio. for the balcony. for
the garden. for the fences. for the tape lines. for the empty
spaces. for the parks. for the post. for the sunshine. for the
rain. for the breeze. for the shade. for the small things. all
the small things. all these small things. every small thing.

Thank you God for the small things,
for the moment,
for the life.

Thank you God I am alive.
Please, God, keep us alive.
Please, God.

Please, God.
Please, God.
Please.

Angels in a Time of Crisis

I've been wondering about angels, recently;
how are they coping, with the influx?

There have been plagues like this in the past,
did they dust off the manual?

Pull out the pages on the Black Death,
and call up the waiting?

Do the angels do night shifts?
Is it ever night, in Heaven?

Do they hold hands with the weary?
Peel off masks, and gowns, and glasses,
and welcome them in?

Do the angels cry for them?
For the joy they're about to experience,
and the loss they've had to endure?

Can angels cry?

And do you think God gives them overtime?
Pays them a bonus of celestial light,
or promises an hour's rest from the endless singing?

Do you think there are any angels left, on Earth?
Or have they all returned home,
to join the welcoming committee?

Stratus

I wish my love were here right now,
I never saw her go;
she died when I was miles away,
for days I didn't know.

I got a call at ten past three
to say that she had died,
and walked for miles to be alone
in empty countryside.

I watched the clouds become a sheet,
the sheet became the sky.
I wondered what it said of God,
that we must always die.

Like Gardening

There is nothing to do but continue. Place your hands
in the grip of a stranger, and guide them on.

In the future we will place life into this earth, place
the goodness we have found here deep into the soil.

With gentle hands, we will bring all that is lost back
into the world. Green shoots uncoil from the darkness.

We will plant this grief, root it deep into the ground,
treat it with wary respect, and see if it flowers.

Though the petals choose their own colours,
let us tend them anyway, and hope that they bloom.

Video Calling the Dead

We're all communicating at a distance, these days.
I wonder, if I call enough times,
will I get through to Heaven?

Between the crackle and hum of the video static
I find you, holding hands with a single angel.
She says, as they always do; *be not afraid.*

And the words are like supernovas, and gas clouds;
each syllable packed with the memory of watching
God breathe it all into being.

You nod your head, and the angel smiles.
My eyeballs shiver, not out of fear, or love, exactly,
but something else.

And as the impossible connection falls away,
I know that you are loved,
and that I am loved,

and I am no longer afraid.

For a Short While

People like to write about Icarus,
but we forget that he flew,
for a short while, anyway;

and people like to write about Judas,
but we forget that he walked with God,
for a short while, anyway;

and people like to write about death,
but forget that we live,
for a short while, anyway;

and perhaps such things
are worth it, are worth
throwing it all away;

oh, what I'd give
to touch such dreams,
for a short while, anyway.

In Silence, Everything

Every night I reach out my soul
as if it's inching its way towards God:

Oh Lord, lift my knees from this dirt,
I am dying so slowly, as we all
must die, and wish to reach you –
to reach you even before I am gone.

If words were hands, there's an army
beating at your gates.

They clamour so loudly they do not see
the walls past the gate posts are rubble.

Lord, where is the grace in this?
In spending a life obsessed with redemption?
There are so many hands on my shoulders
I can barely breathe.

In the silence that sits between words
You place all that has ever been.

All of This is Worship

The plague is happening.
The plague is happening and
services cannot happen in churches.
The plague is happening and
the law says we can only pray
                              privately.

On Saturdays I walk an hour to church.
It is winter now and I bow my head
to the rain. There is a leak before the pulpit,
and someone changes out the bucket. We open
the great door, lean it ajar, to allow people in.
Hang signs on the railings with zip ties.
Church open
                Church open
Sometimes people come in.

The traffic outside keeps circling.
Often there are sirens.
The plague is happening
and we wear masks
and there are sirens
and sometimes people come in.

I trim the candles on the altar.
Dig out the Advent hangings.
Nobody touches.
Nobody moves closer.

Ian, parishioner here for an entire lifetime,
reminds us how things should be.
How they have always been.
How they will be again.

There is a break in the rain and I climb
up to the roof, searching, again, for the leak.
We change out the bucket. Again.
Though we've swept the leaves
from the path we will soon do it again.
Things keep breaking.
Things are always fixed.

I cradle a candle in the crook of my arm,
carve slivers of coloured wax from its base.
Three purple, a pink, and a white.
The stand they will soon fit in is crusted in wax;
leave it, the priest says – *it's a reminder.*

None of the candles stand straight
in the stand we found – but that's okay.
The Christmas tree was crushed
a decade ago, and it doesn't stand straight
either. Nothing is straight at St Nick's.

Someone comes in to pray, the rainbow
flag flutters in the breeze from outside.
Ian plays the organ, simply because he can.

I run my hand over these ancient stones.
Lean back in a pew. Watch the sunlight
play across the nave. Listen to the rain.
The sirens. The organ. Watch as someone
raises a duster, built out of garden canes,
feathers, and duct tape. See them knock the dust
from the tops of the archways. Hear the hoover
as it moves through the vestry. Watch the tea lights
flicker on the stand we found for the grieving.

The plague is happening.
The plague is happening and services
cannot happen in churches.

But this
            all of this is worship.

Plague Baptism

This October we shivered with the loss of it.
With the plague prowling at every door
rebirth means a lot, but more,
it just means a minute or two of light
and water and a recreation of Easter –
when death is bearing down, why wait for dawn?
Each day in our deeds, we are reborn
so just once, in this chaos of death,
let us make this love literal.

Holy Chaos

For Karen Rooms

She reaches out and hauls us in
by our frayed edges,
hands us candles,
says, *you can do this;*

believe.

Throws us the keys,
points out the drawer of silver,
turns her back;

take what you need.

So we lift out the chalice –
in the fading light it gleams,
then we place it on the altar;
taking offerings of peace.

What I Couldn't See

The hardest part is realising You were there for it all,
even in that death-dive, drawing into myself;
the fevered spiral, the ill health, the nothing else.

You were there when the night fell, saw
the beating of flesh, the empty stomach,
the microcosm of madness, the bloody tile.

You were there for the hate crimes and the filthy
pavements. The broken lips, the shouting out for
something, anything. This icy trembling, empty aching,
the bits of myself that are tucked, shaking, away.

You lived through the memories I groomed over,
that I buried deep; slipped beneath smiles and haircuts
and well-fitting but overworn outfits. There's no fooling You.

You witnessed the things I won't even say
in confession. Done when I was yet to see Your care.
You stood beside me, grieving as I called out –

begging for a God already there.

Without Words

We pray this prayer when words will never do,
and in the end God answers,
                              just the same:

A matched beam of love and pain,
and craving, craving, craving
                              at the heart of it.

Golden Golgotha

even when we
wreathe Him in gold
He is still dying

here is our God
on a cross awaiting
the birds

sometimes
He is beautiful, like
we wish we were

sometimes
He is more human
than we

either way
there is blood
and iron

spear shunts
and scratches
and screams

some say this
is a form of
agony

to see God
as broken as
we'll all be

but where else
in the ashes of
creation

will I ever
see a God
who weeps

like me

Atheist out of Necessity

I make sure he is seated by the door,
kept ajar in case he needs to run.
Brother, you are not alone in this;
the Church has an empire of
wrongs weaved into its being
and sometimes there is no going back.

But I found God in these shivering pages
and They're better than this.

Better than petty politics,
bishops in Parliament,
homeless hunched in church doorways –
better than the bleak bigots
bellowing bullshit in town centres
and boys' bedrooms
and behind blocked doorways,
built up as if to say:

There is no way out, not as you,
not like this – become normal.

When was God ever *normal*?
When did God ever make
a rational decision?
Tell me, where in the Bible is sanity?
It must be well hidden
for I have read it a dozen times,
and all I see is the beauty.

I see wonder and love and
holy, holy, holy chaos.

I see boys becoming bearers
of a new way of being,
miracles from dirt
beside seas and in cities –

where in the mountains of Galilee
did you see *normality*?

I saw God with the outcasts
on dusty roads –
and now I'm here in this church
making watery oaths,
and he's there by the door,
headphones on,
blocking out the sermon
for his own sanity.
Once choir boy,
now atheist out of necessity,
but still here for me.

And when you think
of his presence like that –
Isn't it holy?

The Church of Middle England

You're welcome until you're homeless.
Until you're drugged up, or drug dealing.
Welcome until you're angry, or angsty,
or anything other than sane.

Welcome until your accent is cut-throat,
not cut-glass. Until you have to pass
on the collection plate, too skint to chase
a penny from out the margins.

Welcome until your mistakes are
put on paper; a penance of prohibition
even prayer cannot erase. Until this
grace is too much for the mighty.

Welcome until it's harder to let you in
than keep you out. Until the questions
you carry are a gospel of sound. Until your
words become a threat to the easy.

Until calling the Kingdom threatens the peace,
these passed-over prophets call power to cease;
these structures you've built would be trampled
beneath the levelling might of our Saviour's feet.

Abide with us, Lord Jesus,

in the bleak earth, mould-dirt,
in the tent and the tenement
and the cold corner
we found for ourselves.

Dwell amongst us in the ashes,
in the filth and the fright and
the freezing fear of eviction
that comes with each knock at the door.

Make your home in the
dust-dark doorways
of dilapidated factories
and dissipated department stores.

Our endless prayer: *Come, Lord.*

Holy! Holy! Holy!

If God is everywhere, then everywhere is holy,
every*thing* is holy, every*one* is holy.
The blaspheming tongue – holy.
The maze of streets – holy.
The broken street light that flickers on at 2am
to welcome home the dying – it too, is holy.

The homeless are prophets and saints
as much as these bones and fragments.
Treat them with reverence and love them
for they are as holy as any other.
I am holy. You are holy.
The spit that flecks your lips as you curse out a stranger
is disgusting, but holy.

We are disgusting, but holy.

When we leave strangers to die
we are leaving the holy.
When we abandon the lost
we abandon the holy.

Take your neighbour in hand,
lead them to a crowded A&E,
see the doctors pull on their gloves;
the gloves are holy.
The hospital is holy.
The cracked linoleum and buzzing vending machine;
Holy! Holy! Holy!

To save a life, is holy.
All life is holy.

Lord, even death can be holy,
when a person is ready to go.

St Margaret's Bus Station

On the walk to work
he passes the church,
scoops his hands through
the grit in his pockets
for the last of the change;

sits half slant on a seat
in the bus station bay,
and with hands still
deep in his pockets,
begins to pray.

Consider the Sparrows

There ain't no sparrows,
not round here, not anymore.
The cityscape doesn't like
such small resistance.

They're too frail, too
beautiful, too hungry
for a place like this.

So I consider the pigeons
as I perch on the pavement,
myself half-ready for flight.

These city birds;
half-footed, skinny as sin,
pecking in endless circles
at the edge of this concrete earth.

They're not like their siblings,
those set off with the sparrows
someplace beyond the grey.

I heard out there in the fields
you'll see pigeons like baubles,
round and fat and
hanging on every tree.

God is a Capitalist

God's on Spotify now.
God's on YouTube.
God's on Netflix.
God's doing a series
on Amazon Prime.

God is a capitalist.
God cuts down forests
to print Bibles.
God puts palm oil
in the bake sale.
God wraps plastic
round the hosts.

God wants injustice
instead of protests.
God wants nukes
and executions.
God kills the innocent
and says they're guilty.
God hates kindness,
and calls it weakness.

God sings hymns
based on sermons,
based on books,
based on Bibles,
based on old
mistranslations.

God got lost
in this translation.

The Edge of a Past Horizon

I was standing in the sea, of course,
drowning my sorrows by the sand.
The land wasn't made for men like me,
for those made monsters
manipulated into madness,
men told we had this sickness
that maybe the waves could wash clean.

I leaned towards the light out there
on the edge of the horizon,
the skies on the edge of observation,
a blacker blue than my own;
the tone of my voice wavering slightly
as I said these ocean prayers:

Lord wash these waves over me
cleanse me completely,
catch me up in this buoyant sea
and wash me out to greet thee
in the light that floats out there;
untethered by the weather
and the squalls that fill the air.

Was this a prayer, or a portent?
Was drowning what I meant
or the desire to see completely
what the Lord meant for me,
in God we're held eternally
and in that promise we are free;
the hands of God aren't bondage,
but guides that help us truly see
the people we were made to be.

And stepping softly from the sea
the sand scraped all the fear from me,
this salt, this cold, this honesty;
I drew the waves deep into me
and by their rhythm came to see
the man that I was made to be;

so maybe, in the end it's true
that we are guided by
the hand of God, though yet unseen,
we live beneath Their eye,
and if we squint a little
at the edge of sea and sky,
the horizon shines like every star
exploding as we die.

And Repeat

Take this.
> I say, thrusting my hands
> towards the altar.

They seem empty,
> but God knows
> they are full.

Take this. Take this.
I have no time. I have
so little time.

> *Please.*

We Pause at the Red Diamond

What is a person but prayer
disconnected from speech,

our liturgy our lives,
from birth to death.

Come, pray with me a while;
this service is long,

as it must be, and soon
we shall have to depart. ◆

I never killed a man, but it was close

When I dig up my past
I'll bring lead and stone to rebury it.
Iron spikes. Holy water.
Soil from the foot of the cross.
Anything, literally anything
that they say will keep it dead.

I've asked witches and priests
for advice and I think that I'm ready.
Ready enough to bear witness
to all that has been.
To open the grave without
bringing back what I've killed.

Some things are acts of grace
only after they're buried.

I'll take one look into this grave
and make sure I remember it all;
sear the skull of myself into the
back of my eyeballs. Remember:
Knowledge does not equal shame,
but some sins should not be forgotten.

Let the rot be known and noted,
after all, it is myself.
It may have lived, or something similar,
once.
Hear this promise,
these words found at the font:

Whatever I find in that grave
will not see the resurrection.

Graveyard Earth

There's no death in church anymore,
they've carpeted over the gravestones,
slipped Christ from off the cross,
and sprinkled in the jewels:

Rubies, they say, *are red,*
isn't that enough?

I cut myself trimming candles,
red smeared against white wax.
Run it under the tap. *(Notice:*
this church is not connected

to the sewage system, please do
not pour chemicals down this sink)

This red, suspended in tiny swirls –
like rubies, I guess – or wine –
swishes away into the darkness. Blood
returns again, to this graveyard earth.

Ratby Nunnery

The Nuns are leaving.
They sell the cookware
and the furniture.
Call the handyman in from the orchard,
to carry out the pews.

Last year he fixed the guttering,
rabbit-proofed the vegetable patch,
fought a holy war on rats,
and landscaped the lawn.

This year he fills up boxes
with effigies from empty rooms,
sending Jesuses to Africa,
to war with older gods.

When he is done he pockets a crucifix
and locks the gates –
they leave nothing to remember them
in these barren rooms,
but some stained glass,
a brass plaque,
and an apple tree in bloom.

In the Silence

We meet God in the silence, where else
would be big enough to hold that fire form?
That pillar of cloud. That hint of human
that Moses saw, when he said that God
stood before him, on feet just like ours,
and did not raise His hand against him.

Seeking Trans Ancestors in Old Provincial Graveyards

The dead are calling out again;
I heard their names the other day,
rarely spoken beyond the edge
of the graveyard – unconsecrated
ground cannot hold them for long.
There are names and names and
empty syllables *'until the day break'*.
Every day breaks like a man,
and every night falls like a woman,
and the dawn arises and the moon
in the daytime hangs silent and awkward,
like the rest who've never belonged.

And they hang pride flags outside the churches
now, and the homophobes claim it's God's rainbow,
and the queers claim it's our rainbow, and God claims
all of us anyway, long before we are born.

In the wind I hear the names
again. Their echoes are all the syllables
we've never quite said. Dead. Undead.
Dead. Undead. Dead. Undead.
Until the day break I walk the church line,
drag my feet over endless graves,
speak the names. All these empty
names. Those too weathered
to read, I speak loudest
of all. A response call. *Joshua.*
Edward. Mary. Beloved of her family.
Born. Lived. *Died.* A date. A promise. A fall.

Christianity for Heathens

i.
Love everyone as if everyone is holy,
as if everyone's intrinsically worthy,
as if the streets are strewn with Christ
taking naps in empty doorways.

ii.
Love yourself as if you are loved,
as if you were never an accident,
as if everything you were meant to be
waits for you to claim it.

iii.
Love the world as if it were a gift,
as if you were made as part of it,
as if you were meant to tend to it –
every inch of earth is Holy Ground.

iv.
Love justice, and kindness, and truth,
as if everything depends on it,
as if everything depends on it.
Everything depends on it.

v.
You were given a gift, and trusted.
Love it all, love it all,
love it always.

?.
Know this, if you know anything at all:
Life is no challenge, nor test;
life is love.

∞.
Reflect it back in abundance.

You Eat God?!

I said,

       You eat God?!

They said,

       We eat God, *together*

I said,

       You *eat* God?!

They said,

       God feeds us, we gather

I said,

       But you *do* eat God?!

They said,

       God is more than this

They said,

       Here, *take this bread*

Just Talk About the Weather

They told me not to swear at the bishop,
I said not to worry,
said I knew small talk when I saw it,
said, *what a shitty day for a party;*
it's pissing it down out there.
Did it fuck up your fancy hat?

All Creatures

The rats attend church
               sometimes,
sat at the back
in shifting lines.

Who needs church mice
when you can go bigger?

Who needs church mice
when the church rats
come shining out the canal
every Sunday;

sit themselves
on the prayer books,
chitter along to the hymns:

All Creatures of our God and King

eyes wide and clever,
watching everything.

The Altar Frontal at St Nick's is a Rainbow Flag

There is nothing special about this church;
people cluster in pews, partners, friends, a few
families for good measure. A toddler cries.
His mothers rise to a squat, hold his hands,
walk him slowly round the aisles. They circle the font
where he was baptised alongside one of his mothers.

The priest holds up the wafer, the chalice;
papers rustle, this order of service. An ambulance
rushes by, the organ begins to breathe; its song
is older than we are. Come now, rise; approach
this altar. The body of Christ. The blood of Christ.
The fellowship of Christ. These signs of peace.

This Body

This body is a cathedral holier than those
made by human hands. This body is a
cathedral holier than those made by
human hands. This body is undergoing
a personal reformation. This body is
enduring a modern iconoclasm.
This body is being remade in a new
shade of beauty. This body is altering
its archways. This body is reverting
old changes. This body is fixing the
damage. This body is filled with prayer.
This body holds relics of saints. This body
turns sunlight to statuary. This body is
built out of bondage. This body is still
a cathedral. This body is still holy.
This body is filled with worship.
We cense these shattered bones.

In Search of St Sebastian

They say hello like it's
who let you in here,

accusation turned admonition
turned grudging admiration;

> *how dare you come here,*
> *and how brave of you*
> *to dare.*

In the stained glass I am searching for
a saint writhes – naked and pained.

It's said if you stand on the pew and
line it up – just right – you'll see yourself;

> somehow both dying
> and daring, in the agony
> of his eyes.

Martyrdom

Being Queer shouldn't get us killed
but   ,   ;
                    ,
                          ?
      ,   -   ;

                  (   )   ,
            ,   -
                    ,   ;

      ,   ?

The Love of God; The Loss of Church

i.
They accept the fist until it opens,
until the splayed flesh
shows the difference.

We can watch a hundred sinners,
say these self-appointed saints,
but you,

        Sister,   *Darling,*

not dying now, but daring,
you've turned into something else
entirely.

ii.
Turn, Brother, and take your leave.

Shake the dust of their hearts
from the soles of your feet,

there's a God out here far bigger
than the best of them.

Jay

The words You speak sound
like birdsong. When You call
out my name, it is
like the dawn.

This is the name You gave
before I claimed it. Spoken
before anyone
was born.

Like Thomas

I have been building myself
out of scraps of shattered dreams;
God hands me flour and water,
says: *I know what it's like.*

The surgeons say I have only to
count backwards from ten
and when I wake I will be reborn.

And reborn I touch
my own body for the first time;
incredulous at the miracle
right before my eyes.

Show Me How To Love

O Lord show me how to love,

how to form my body like water
against the skin of another.

How to hold my heart in my hand,
how to offer it to another man;
how to say:

I love you so much
I would risk the whole world
just to hold you.

                    Show me how
to embrace all that You made me
in the image of all that You are.

How to delve deep inside my soul,
how to see myself whole;
how to witness in all of this love

the unblemished work of God.

Addressing the Backlog

There are acres of filing cabinets
on the edges of Heaven, filled with:
Why, God, Why, God? Why?

       Because   is not an answer,
nor, God admits, is it *the* answer –
but what else can They say?

Nine Altars

The east end of Durham Cathedral is not the same
style as everywhere else, do we even see it?
Do we grasp the edges of these vast windows,
pull them down, force them smaller, fix their curves
until they *fit*? Do we tear off the marble?
Scrub at the carvings? Do we condemn the Gothic
until it's Norman again? Do we unhinge our mouths
and swallow the statues? Thump our fists against
the lines in the floor that show where the last east end
stood? Do we beg it to rise back out of the earth?
Demand the return of the original incarnation,
proven unfit for purpose or pilgrimage? Or do we
stand in silence, staring at the scale of such a thing?
Do we barely notice the change? So caught up in
this sense of wonder, that such beauty exists at all.

Cathedralsong

It is night and I am watching the cathedral;
like an avid twitcher, I identify every wing.

Look! There she sits – see the shadows of the
floodlights, the curved details; that romanesque
flourish, splicing into gothic, into grandeur, into …

                                                    gone.

She's flying into dreams again, each stone
a compendium of prayer. First formed
by the hands of men long dead, yet still
she speaks; song and silence synthesised
into the sound of the sacred. She is
an instrument of interpolation; an organ
built entirely of time – each life that is lived
adds syllables to centuries of song.

Like any good twitcher, I see by silhouette;
move slowly, so as not to scare her off.

Listen closely, now – each cathedral sings
with a slightly different sound.

Ruins

Coventry Cathedral Part I

                    Sometimes
you walk in these bombed-out ruins and feel
the edges of the past align, like fragments of
shattered glass in the shifting sun; and somehow
you can taste the rain that fell before the falling,
see those who lived before the dying, know the
beauty that's here beneath the scorching; and
in these stones, worn with love and loss and life,
you feel this fire –   O! There was fire!

Reconciliation

Coventry Cathedral Part II

           What you hold on to
doesn't have to be this; heat-kissed stonework and
fallen beams, these overthrown certainties do not
require rebuilding.

           Repair the damage
without renewing all that has been; some losses
must be seen to be accepted.

           Let us learn to forgive,
let us build an edifice that speaks of this; let us turn
this shattering to sunlight, and preach a promise
of peace.

Come Down

The joy destroys her, see:
Trace the cracks with our fingertips;
a tale of trauma stretched across stone.

One day the bells shall ring,
the tower shall shift too far,
shall shed this structural integrity,

this ancient ingenuity;
stones shaken apart
by centuries of sound.

But that day is not today;
and the bells cry out into chaos,
saying: there is love here,

come listen.
      Come listen.
            Come down.

Scriptorium

Take oak tree and calf,
split them apart;

gall and skin and bark,
and in them the whole world;

all our knowledge curled
on sheaves of skin.

Sharpen your quills,
wring ink from out the trees.

Harness all this death
to write our own eternities.

In Memoriam

He scratches a hole in the dirt
and places his thumb in it,
knuckle deep;

tips a shower of seeds into
his filthy palm, and
counts:

A child's prayer, a burn-marked Bible,
a shattered window, a siren,
a song, a silence;

placed into the earth in neat lines,
not so close that one would
kill the other.

Ten years from now this earth will
still bloom at the edges of
every winter,

each unfolding flower
a tiny act
of grace.

Graves like Gardens

There must be a place in the world
where they treat gravediggers like gardeners;
planting bodies like bulbs and seeing what grows.

It's not as strange as it seems, you know;
there's a reason the grass in the graveyard
is always so green.

God in the Garden

Before he died
he saw God in the garden.
Said She came in a nightdress
like the one his mother wore,
in those hungry years after the war
when everyone was grieving.

And She walked over ice
without leaving a print,
and She reached out her hands
and they coiled like springs,
and She looked like every woman
he'd ever known, all at once –
so unremarkable She was startling.

He said that all the places
She walked the grass grew
higher than before; even showed
me the circles of green in the lawn,
with blades of grass
like wheat.

Before Creation

In the beginning there was nothing,
not even nothing.
Nothing is the absence of something
and something hadn't yet been.

In the beginning there was just God.
God wasn't floating,
because floating requires something
to float in, and there wasn't any of that,
not yet.

Nor was God standing,
for reasons covered above.
There being nothing to stand on,
or in, or under, or next to.

In the beginning, there was just God.
God being God.
Doing God things
on a plane of existence
we cannot comprehend.

But one day,
(though there were no days,
not just yet)
God spoke
and wove the world into being.

Palm Sunday

One day soon they will ask what this means
as He enters the city on a donkey, for peace;
neither brought by a warhorse, or by His feet,
on a path strewn with cloaks with palm leaves beneath.

And the chaos He causes is a seismic event,
there's no need to make speeches when you're heaven sent;
and the leaders and rulers, on the walls, half bent,
look down at this Man in triumphal lament.

He wept for the city, and now that He's near
He rides without speaking, and still the crowd cheer,
clamouring loudly through danger and fear:
The prophet called Jesus is here! He is here!

His presence is preaching, but no one can know
the reason He's come or the way that He'll go,
and today He just rides, gentle and slow,
down the road, through the gates, over palm leaves,

      and so –

when they look at this day, beginning to see
the ways He fulfills each of these prophecies,
they'll notice a quietness, beyond all belief:
God claiming this kingdom, without having to speak.

Up and Out in Gethsemane

There's a garden named Gethsemane
with olive trees tangled like thorns –
each branch crooked – reaching up and out
at the same time, like every one of our prayers;
alternating syllables edged between Heaven
and Earth.

One day a Man came, and His prayers
cradled all of creation, before falling back
into Himself; up and out at the same time.
And He was raised, up and out at the same time.
And we were saved, up and out at the same time;
replayed:

> a scrap of bread in the hands of a priest
> who will never see this garden. Up and out.
> Raised and distributed like prayer;
> all of us rising and reaching,
> edged between Heaven
> and Earth.

Vox Pops from Golgotha

When the temple cracked I cried out,
having been halfway to laughing when it happened;
spear slung low and dripping this cooling blood.

                    – But it's a living, I guess. It's a living.
And in ten years of crucifying criminals,
I only killed God *once*.

Mary Magdalene and the Gardener

At first Mary thought He was a gardener,
this miraculous Son.
She saw the dirt under His nails
through the tears in her eyes,
and saw not the grave, but the bringer of life;

And how was she wrong, then?

This woman wrapped in grief,
who saw the dirt of a borrowed tomb,
and thought at first of things which bloom;
Which turn their heads to the sun,
and burst into joyous colour.

The Carpenter

He knew his son
would outshine him
from the beginning,

so taught this child the
only thing he could:

The skill of taking
blades and wood,

and turning death
into something
else entirely.

In Persona Christi

The priest is texting me at 2am.
The priest is texting me, and he is lonely,
and he is lovely, and it is dark.
The priest is texting at 2am
and remembering when he wasn't a priest;
remembering when he didn't believe.

The priest is texting me and saying,
tomorrow I have to be Jesus, that's
what they say about priests, you know?
They say we stand in for Jesus.
Can you imagine the pressure?

I imagine him becoming Jesus.
Imagine him slipping into scarred skin
hands curling gently around a chisel,
around another hand,
around the edges of the dying.
I imagine him reaching out and up
and lifting the death clean out of us.

I imagine that the edges of his
vestments are lined with dirt,
from the walk, you know?
From the journey.

And I imagine him holding himself
in his own palms, broken now and whole,
putting himself into himself into himself;
breaking himself into pieces in front of a crowd.

He tears his body in two,
saying: these crumbs, they are me,
and these hands, they are me,
and these people, they are me,

and this Spirit, it is me,
and this God, it is me,
and this me, I am me.
I am more me than me
but not less.

And he holds himself at the altar
placing himself into others,
placing himself into others,
placing himself into himself,
every piece of himself;
until there's a moment –
where he stands in a sea of silence
and knows it has all been consumed.

Late Night Theology

I remember sitting up one night
so late that it was morning
in the guest room of a vicarage
in a city that wasn't mine.

I was thinking about how God saw time,
how it probably wasn't a line
but a single point;
like everything that ever happened
was condensed into a moment,
and that nothing really ever happen*ed*
because everything was always happen*ing*.

I thought that moment probably went on forever,
and for no time at all,
and everything we were and are and would be
was all squished deep inside,
like a tree inside a seed.

And I remember trying to explain this at 7am,
before the Vicar had even said morning prayer,
how the idea of it filled the air,
and I showed him all of history
condensed in a single point.

and I guess that's why,
I remember saying,
I guess that's why, sometimes,
God just Takes Their Time.

He bowed his head, took a long gulp
of his morning coffee, and said:
there's a book on this in the living room
go argue such things with the saints.

The First Sunday

On the seventh day God rested,
placed Her feet on the coffee table,
leaned back in Her favourite armchair,
and turned on the news.

The angels, scrolling ticker-tape
across the bottom of the screen
repeated the only words to be found:
Everything. Everything. Everything.

Everything is new. Everything is news.
At a time as yet unspecified,
        (because time had not begun)
Elohim created.

                Elohim created,
and everything was new.
She sighed, and invented sighing,
before closing Her eyes.

Late into that long morning,
to a backing track of celestial snoring,
the angel behind the newsdesk
was still explaining the concept of sky.

Splitting Fares

because I love you / I'll tell you how this goes / one day you will meet a man / and the man will promise you / everything / and you will ask the man / if he is God / and he will laugh and say / *there is no God* / and you will nod politely and drink cocktails // and in the taxi home / the stranger you're splitting the fare with will ask / *how did it go with that laughing man* / and you will answer / *nothing is less attractive / than laughter directed at faith* / and she will smile / and maybe it's the street lights / but her pupils flash / like flames // and when she places her hand / on the seat between you / you take it without thinking / and you see the driver / has a halo / and the roadway / is the cosmos / and when she kisses your forehead / it feels like the meaning of love // and when you arrive / when the taxi pulls up outside your house / you will ask her if she will come in / for a coffee / for a tea / for a glass of water / for anything at all / and she will smile / and you will question all you have seen / until she speaks:

> *I am already there with you*
> *Don't you see?*
> *I always have been*

and the taxi will drive off / the exhaust rattling / a little over the road / perhaps when you're in church tomorrow / you'll spot her off in the corner enjoying the show / and you'll swear her eyes flicker at every /   *AMEN*

Knowing the Unknowable

God and Time are concepts I'll never quite get
how they interact and yet, one created the other.
Time is king, but Time's Mother straddles the stars,
She vaults the asteroid belt and swims
through Saturn's slipstream, just to meet us.

When I ask priests about how it all works
they smile wryly and say *some things are
simply unknowable. There's some books
on this on the table, but none of them ever agree.*

At the lych gate I stumbled across a Woman,
smoke pouring from Her mouth, without
cigarette, Her eyes fires, Her lips wet.
She smiled, and leaned forward slightly,
saying, *I believe I can answer your question.*

And the Word She spoke in that place
was the one that brought Time into being.

An Angel in Baker Street Station

I saw an angel in Baker Street Station once.
I rushed down the steps and there it was,
floating some twelve feet above the tracks,
shifting and shining and somehow every shape
all at once, and a dozen, a hundred, a myriad
eyes, all staring in every direction.

And when the man on the platform stepped
forward, arms spread out towards the train
that was just now rushing out of the tunnel like a
furious tongue, the wind of its arrival pushed him
back again. Pushed him back again, and he fell.
Spine striking the pavement.

Around him no one was moved, and the angel
blinked out of existence. The train stopped.
A woman in a neon jacket clattered down the steps
can I help you? she asked, *can I help?*
She placed an arm under his and lifted.
A glimpse of golden light hit the floor.

Dag Gadol

I am standing at the back of the bookstore;
Jonah is signing copies of his autobiography,
the miraculous isn't all it's cracked up to be,

                                why can't they see it?

                     It's just a big fish!
I shout from the doorway:

                          Just one massive fish!
          Stop saying it's a whale!

Jonah looks up at me, slips the lid of his pen from his lips,
and cracks a smile;

             and what is it, do you think, about fish,
that would make this any less   *of a miracle?*

The Volunteer

He walked in quietly,
saw me sweeping the
leaves from the porch
and picked up a broom;

and he smiled as he worked,
carefully clearing the mud
beneath each of the pews.

He didn't give a name
but whistled, softly,
stopping out of respect
if someone came in.

It was only afterwards,
when he handed
back the broom

that I saw the scars:
bursts of white like stars,
blazing out from the centre
of each palm.

Multi-Story

Jesus sits on the edge of the car park;
robes hitched to His knees, He swings His legs
to and fro against the concrete. I say, *Lord,*

you'll scrape your skin on these stones.

My Son, He says – for He calls me Son,
unlike any Father I've had before – *if death
could not best these bones, why would this?*

I point out the cathedral in the distance:
*See that house we made you, a thousand years past?
There's a throne for you there, and a man who*

keeps it warm, shall we go?

He doesn't speak, just looks out at the city.
A car backfires. A baby cries. And the sunset lights
His flyaway hairs, like a shining circle of thorns.

Jesus, upon hearing of the death of John the Baptist

He is aching, and the sun on His chest is like gilding
and I wonder if that's how they'll paint Him;
somehow always on the edge of humanity.
The holy only just contained in this fallible flesh.

But He is soft, like we are, and His teeth flash white
against His lips when He speaks, and when the sun
sets – that's when He shifts, slightly, in the long light.
As if, for a moment, He falls away from us,

not deliberately, but by degrees, returning in an
instant to say: *tomorrow we walk on, to the sea,*
where Andrew will catch fish, and later I will
show you how to make a meal that will last

for the ages.

Jesus at the Gay Bar

He's here in the midst of it –
right at the centre of the dance floor,
robes hitched up to His knees
to make it easy to spin.

At some point in the evening
a boy will touch the hem of His robe
and beg to be healed, beg to be
anything other than this;

and He will reach His arms out,
sweat-damp, and weary from dance.
He'll cup this boy's face in His hand
and say,

     my beautiful child
there is nothing in this heart of yours
that ever needs to be healed.

'Queer' is a Calling

They want us to be
ashamed of this, God,
so why did you make us?
Spin stars together
in shapes that never quite

                        fit?

We were called to
complete your creation.
Like the skies
we were shaped
by your song.

Beatitudes for a Queerer Church

Blessed are the outcasts;
the ostracised, the outsiders.

Blessed are the scared;
the scarred, the silent.

Blessed are the broken;
for they are not broken.

Blessed are the hated;
for they are not worthy of hate.

Blessed are those who try;
those who transform, who transition.

Blessed are the closeted;
God sees you shine anyway.

Blessed are the queers;
who love creation enough to live the truth of it,
despite a world that tells them they cannot.

And blessed are those
who believe themselves unworthy of blessing;
what inconceivable wonders you hold.

Poem Acknowledgements

'Ratby Nunnery' was originally published by Troika Books in the 2019 collection *Clouds Cannot Cover Us*.

'Palm Sunday' was originally commissioned by the BBC for the BBC Radio 2 programme *At The Foot of the Cross*, part of their 2021 Good Friday programming.

Thanks

As with all books, this poetry collection would not have been possible without the help and support of a huge number of people. So let us begin the thanks:

To Kym Deyn, who shares my birthday, my need to write poetry, and my chaotic nature; and who turned a rambling three-hour phone call about the 'vibe' of this book into a coherent pitch, as well as being single-handedly responsible for the title of the collection (all of my title suggestions were awful, as you can probably tell by looking at the state of the individual poem titles in this book, which are entirely my fault). It is not an exaggeration to say that this book would not exist without them. I could not wish for a better friend, or a better comrade in poetic nonsense.

To Revd Philippa White, who kindly offered to look through a large number of the poems as my unofficial 'accidental heresy checker'; if any heresy remains, it is entirely my fault, and possibly deliberate. If you consider queer-affirming Christianity 'heresy', that is your problem.

To Alex Bond, the Senior Curator in Charge of Birds at the Natural History Museum, who is a very good egg, and cast his professional ornithological eye over a handful of the poems included here (because I know nothing about birds). If any bird-based errors remain, please chalk them up to poetic licence and metaphor.

To all of the poor unsuspecting priests in churches up and down the country who have found themselves in sudden and unexpected deep conversations with me. As well as being of general theological and pastoral help, many of those conversations sparked poems, and you deserve to be thanked for that.

Finally, I want to thank the Revd Canon Karen Rooms, and everyone at St Nicholas' Church, Leicester. You took me into your ancient inclusive church as a plague raged outside and showed me incredible care and kindness. I have been honoured to find a home here among you, even in such trying times, and without you, and all you have brought to my life, this collection of poems would never have been written. Prepare to be hugged to within an inch of your lives when hugs are legal again.

March 2021

Printed in the USA
CPSIA information can be obtained
at www.ICGtesting.com
LVHW090211240324
775349LV00018B/165